Takehiko Inoue

THE TWO WISHES I HAD WHEN I STARTED WRITING *SLAM DUNK* HAVE BOTH COME TO PASS. THE FIRST WAS TO MAKE A "RESEARCH" TRIP TO THE UNITED STATES FOR THE NBA FINALS. THE SECOND WAS TO SEE THE OLYMPICS IN BARCELONA (MORE RESEARCH!). I'M GRATEFUL THAT BOTH DREAMS CAME TRUE.

MY NEW DREAM IS TO SEE JAPANESE BASKETBALL REPRESENTED AT THE OLYMPICS. IF THERE ARE KIDS ON THAT TEAM WHO FIRST DISCOVERED THE SPORT THROUGH *SLAM DUNK*... I'D BE SO HAPPY I THINK I'D CRY. SERIOUSLY.

Takehiko Inoue's ***Slam Dunk*** is one of the most popular manga of all time, having sold over 100 million copies worldwide. He followed that series up with two titles lauded by critics and fans alike—***Vagabond***, a fictional account of the life of Miyamoto Musashi, and ***Real***, a manga about wheelchair basketball.

SLAM DUNK

Vol. 9: A Team of Troubled Teens

SHONEN JUMP Manga Edition

STORY AND ART BY TAKEHIKO INOUE

English Adaptation/Kelly Sue DeConnick
Translation/Joe Yamazaki
Touch-up Art & Lettering/James Gaubatz
Cover & Graphic Design/Sean Lee
Editor/Kit Fox

VP, Production/Alvin Lu
VP, Sales & Product Marketing/Gonzalo Ferreyra
VP, Creative/Linda Espinosa
Publisher/Hyoe Narita

Printed in the U.S.A.

Published by VIZ Media, LLC
P.O. Box 77010
San Francisco, CA 94107

10 9 8 7 6 5 4 3 2 1
First printing, April 2010

STORY AND ART BY

TAKEHIKO INOUE

SLAM DUNK

Vol. 9: A Team of Troubled Teens

Character Introduction

Hanamichi Sakuragi
A first-year at Shohoku High School, Sakuragi is in love with Haruko Akagi.

Haruko Akagi
Also a first-year at Shohoku, Takenori Akagi's little sister has a crush on Kaede Rukawa.

Takenori Akagi
A third-year and the basketball team's captain, Akagi has an intense passion for his sport.

Kaede Rukawa
The object of Haruko's affection (and that of many of Shohoku's female students!), this first-year has been a star player since junior high.

Sakuragi's Friends

Ohkusu Mito Takamiya Noma

Ryota Miyagi
A problem child with a thing for Ayako.

Ayako
Basketball Team Manager

Hisashi Mitsui
The leader of a rival gang with a grudge against Ryota.

Our Story Thus Far

Hanamichi Sakuragi is rejected by close to 50 girls during his three years in junior high. In high school, he joins the basketball team in order to get closer to his beloved Haruko, whose brother is the team captain. However, the endless fundamental drills do not suit his personality, and he and Captain Akagi frequently butt heads.

After a good showing in their first exhibition game, the team already has its sights set on Nationals when former player and constant troublemaker Ryota Miyagi is released from the hospital and returns to the team.

Miyagi was laid up after a particularly brutal fight with Mitsui and his thugs. Nevertheless, the team is glad to have him back.

Not content to let bygones be bygones, Mitsui and his gang invade the gym and cause a ruckus, during which several players are injured. In the end, it's revealed that Mitsui

Vol. 9:
A Team of Troubled Teens

Table of Contents

72
START
SHOHOKU

HELLO.
HARUKO AKAGI HERE.
朝日生命ビル
I LOVE SUNDAY MORNINGS... ESPECIALLY WHEN IT'S WARM LIKE TODAY.
MMM
THE BASKETBALL TEAM HAS TO PRACTICE ON SUNDAYS. BUT HONESTLY... THEY'RE LUCKY THEY GET TO PRACTICE AT ALL.
THEY'RE LUCKY THE WHOLE TEAM DIDN'T GET SUSPENDED.

READ THIS WAY

H-HEY!!
WHAT'S GOING ON HERE?!

!!

BUSTED.
THINK OF SOME-THING...
THINK OF SOME-THING...
...
UH.........
...
GAH!
I GOT NOTHING'!
SCRITCH SCRITCH
MITSUI SAID HE WAS GONNA LEAVE THE LIFE AND GO BACK TO PLAYIN' IT STRAIGHT ON THE BASKET-BALL TEAM.
I GUESS WE KINDA LOST IT...

...AND WE, UM, JUMPED THEM.
WE JUMPED THE TEAM *AND* MITSUI.
SORRY.

YOU DID *WHAT* ?!

ISN'T THAT RIGHT, HOTTA?
!!
!!
YEAH.
THAT'S RIGHT.
SHUFFLE SHUFFLE SHUFFLE
SORRY.

YOHEI?!

READ THIS WAY

HARUKO!!
JAS

HUH?

THE SUSPENSION SQUAD HAS ARRIVED!
HEY GUYS...
HEE
CHIT
CHAT
MUTTER
HEH HEH HEH!
WASSUP?
YOHEI AND HIS FRIENDS RECEIVED THREE DAYS SUSPENSION.

READ THIS WAY

THEY TOOK THE FALL...
CHATTER
AH HA HA HA
CHATTER
CHATTER
CHATTER
CLEAR
...FOR HANAMICHI AND FOR MITSUI.

LATER, HARUKO!
This is as far as we go!
LATER, FELLAS!

...

PACHI
Today's my lucky day.
You always say that.
HEH HEH
HEH HEH
Ha ha!

ONLY ONE WEEK UNTIL THE TOURNAMENT.

HMPH...

GOOD LUCK!!

C'MON!
I'M OPEN!
SQUEAK
DEFENSE, GUYS!! KEEP PLAYING D!!

SQUEAK
HERE!
SQUEAK
PASS!
SQUEAK
PASS!
SQUEAK
SQUEAK
MIYAGI!!
DON'T YOU GET LAZY ON ME!!
HMPH!
MOVE THOSE FEET!
HEADS UP!!

YOINK
HA!!
!!
DE-NIED!
FLICK
C'MON! D UP!! DON'T LET AKAGI SCORE!!
MM...
CLAP
CLAP
HANDS UP!!
GRR...
AYAKO... ♡
HMPH!

WATCH AND LEARN!!

SLAM

AHH!!

HUFF
HUFF
!

OKAY...
YOU GUYS PLAY D TILL YOU STOP ONE.

WOW...
THE GORILLA DUNK!!
HOOP

READY?

READ THIS WAY

READY AS I'LL EVER BE, MITSUI.
MITSUI CUT HIS HAIR.

HE SWALLOWED HIS PRIDE TO PLAY BASKETBALL.

SQUEAK

IT'S GONNA TAKE SOME TIME FOR THE GUYS TO COME AROUND...

HUFF

HUFF

SQUEAK

SQUEAK

AFTER TWO YEARS, YOU CAN'T JUST PICK UP WHERE YOU LEFT OFF.

PAAAA

BUT I DON'T THINK IT'LL BE LONG BEFORE HE'S AN INTEGRAL PART OF THE TEAM ONCE AGAIN.

FEH! I DON'T RECALL US FORGIVING HIM.

GROUSE

GROUSE

GROUSE

Eh?

YOU'RE WITH ME, EH, YASU? HE CLOCKED US BOTH.

RIGHT?

Er...

I-I'M KINDA OVER IT...

HOOP

GO, MITSUI!!

SWISH

IT'S GOOD !!
GAH!
GAH!

YOUR DEFENSE BITES, KOGURE.

MAYBE HE CAN PICK UP WHERE HE LEFT OFF!
THAT'S WHAT I GET FOR FEELING SORRY FOR HIM!
EEESH!
HUFF
HUFF
HUFF
HUFF
HUFF
HUFF
CAN I GO HOME NOW?

READ THIS WAY

GIMME THE BALL!!
ME! ME! ME! ME!

PAA
INSIDE!! GET INSIDE, HANA-MICHI!!

SAKU-RAGI, DON'T FORGET WHAT I TOLD YOU!
MIND YOUR LEGS!

I KNOW!!
CATCH IT IN MIDAIR ...

...AND LAND ON BOTH FEET!!
TAP
THEN I CAN PIVOT EITHER WAY!!
SQUEAK

AND THE LOW POST IS ALL MINE !!
HUA
AH!!

READ THIS WAY

HI, FELLAS!
I BROUGHT REFRESH-MENTS!!

HARUKO!
Yes!!

DID YOU CATCH THAT?! MY AWESOME AND POWER-FUL LOW POST MANEUVER?!
BONK
MORON!! YOU MISSED!!

GREAT TIMING, HARUKO.
Thanks.
Thanks...
TOURNAMENT'S JUST AROUND THE CORNER, HUH?
HAVE SOME, HANAMICHI.

HOW'S EVERYONE DOING?
ARE YOU KIDDING?
I'M ON A ROLL!
HA HA HA

SWI
TH-
THUMP
!!
LOOKS LIKE RUKAWA'S ON A ROLL... ♡
GRR!
RUKAWA!!
WE'RE STILL PLAYING, *IDIOT*.
THE PREFECTURAL TOURNAMENT IS ALMOST UPON US!
PAA
PAA
SQUEAK
SQUEAK
SQUEAK

...
SNIFF...
SLAM DUNK

#73 MAY 19TH

MAY 19TH
TWEET
TWEET
TWEET

TICK
TOCK
TICK
TOCK
6:00 A.M.
TICK

TICK
TOCK
TICK
TOCK
OOF...
...

CAN'T SLEEP!
SAKURAGI COULDN'T SLEEP ONE WINK.

SHOHOKU
5
11

#73
MAY 19TH
SHOHOKU

HUFF
HUFF
HUFF
TODAY'S THE BIG DAY!!
THE GENIUS SAKURAGI MAKES HIS DEBUT!!
PAT PAT PAT
THE GENIUS LOOSENS UP WITH AN EARLY MORNING JOG...
HEH HEH HEH
THIS IS HOW GENIUSES ROLL!!
The genius lifestyle!
RAAAH
INTRO-DUCING THE STARTING LINEUPS!!
IN THE RED JERSEYS, SHOHOKU HIGH SCHOOL!!
MY DEBUT ...

READ THIS WAY

NUMBER 4!
CLOMP
CLOMP
CLOMP

GORI !!
OOGA
OOGA
BOO!
BOO!
BOO!

BOO!
BOO!
GOOD LUCK, TAKE-NORI!!

UH... THEN THESE THREE GUYS!
PIP PIP PIP
YIP!
OOGA
OOGA
AND THE ONE YOU'VE BEEN WAITING FOR..

KCHUNG

RAH!
EEEEEEEEE!

SHO-HOKU'S NUMBER 10...
YAY!!
RAH!
THE *GENIUS* BASKET-BALLMAN ...
EEEEEEE!!
RAH!
RAH!

HANAMICHIII...
AAAAHHHH
TWINKLE
EEEEEE!
EEEEI!
SAKUUUURAGI!!
EEEEEE!

EH?
EEEEE!

HOW DID SHE GET DOWN THERE?!
HANAMICHI!!
ACK!

I'M SCARED, HANA-MICHI...
YOU'RE SUCH A HUGE STAR...
SNIFF
RAH!
RAH!
RAH!

HANA-MICHI! ♡

HARU-KO...
TWINKLE
THE ONLY FAN WHO MATTERS TO ME IS YOU.

READ THIS WAY

EEP!
H-
HARUKO!

HANA-
MICHI...
♡
I'm so happy.
YIP!
HARUKO
...

IN THE
CHEERING
CROWD,
THE ONLY
VOICE I
HEAR—
MUMBLE
MUMBLE
HANA-
MICHI?

'MORNING.
AM I
INTRUDING?
NO...
NO!!

SO
TODAY'S
THE BIG
DAY...
YOU
GUYS ARE
GONNA DO
GREAT.
PAT
PAT
PAT
OH
YEAH?

YES! SHE
KNOWS A
GENIUS
WHEN SHE
SEES
ONE!!

ZOOM
YEAH! GETTING RUKAWA WAS BIG!
For Shohoku.
SUPER ROOKIE!
GE-NIUS.
!!

OH?
SURE, RUKAWA MIGHT HELP A LITTLE, BUT...
HA HA HA
C'MON! HE'S STILL A JUNIOR HIGH PLAYER, REALLY.
He's not all that.

WELL, IF YOU ASK ME, SHOHOKU HAS THREE OF THE PREFECTURE'S VERY BEST.
THE VERY BEST?!

YEAH...

#4 Takenori Akagi
(Third-Year)
197cm 90kg※
Position: Center

※ 6'6" and 198 lbs.

PAAA

PAAA

SWISH

HUFF...

AT LAST...

#7 Ryota Miyagi
(Second-Year)
168cm 59kg※
Position: Point Guard

ZHHHHHH

※ 5'6" and 130 lbs.

HUFF...

...

MWAH
'MORNING, AYAKO! ♡
WISH ME LUCK! ♡

#11 Kaede Rukawa
(First-Year)
187cm 75kg※
Position: Forward

※ 6'2" and 165 lbs.

WHOO—SH

READ THIS WAY

ZOOOOM

HUH?

CRASH
!!
Whoa!

HUM DE DUM..
JANGLE
T·A·I·Z·O
LAWSON

WHAT THE—?!
...
Jeepers ...

THOSE THREE ARE THREE OF THE **BEST PLAYERS** IN THE PREFECTURE.
Hands down...
POUT!
...

WAIT! ONE MORE!
!!
YOU REMEMBERED!
The genius!

MITSUI.
D'OH!

#14 Hisashi Mitsui
(Third-Year)
184cm 70kg※
Position: Shooting Guard

※ 6' and 154 lbs.

...

...
HNNN

READ THIS WAY

I CAN DO THIS!!
Nice teeth...

SHOHOKU'S GOT A REALLY SOLID TEAM THIS YEAR!
PLUS ...
HARUKO...
WE HAVE YOU.
TWITCH
!

I GOT YOU TO JOIN THE TEAM...
...AND I HAVE AN EYE FOR TALENT!!
HEE HEE
...
HARUKO...

YOU HAVE AN EYE FOR **GENIUS**!!

RAH
RAH
RAH
市体育館

Scoreboard: Shohoku 1st Half 2nd Half Miuradai

LET'S GO!!

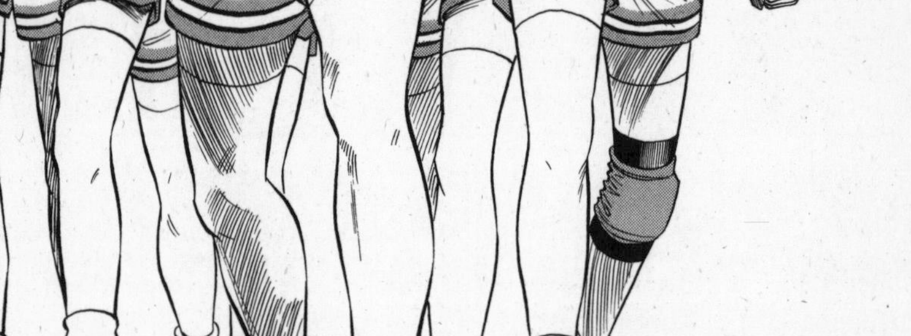

HERE COMES SHOHO-KU!!
RAH
AKAGI'S HUGE!!
RAH
THEY ONLY LOST TO RYONAN BY ONE POINT?!
RAH
WHO'S BIG RED?!
WHOA!

YEAH !!!

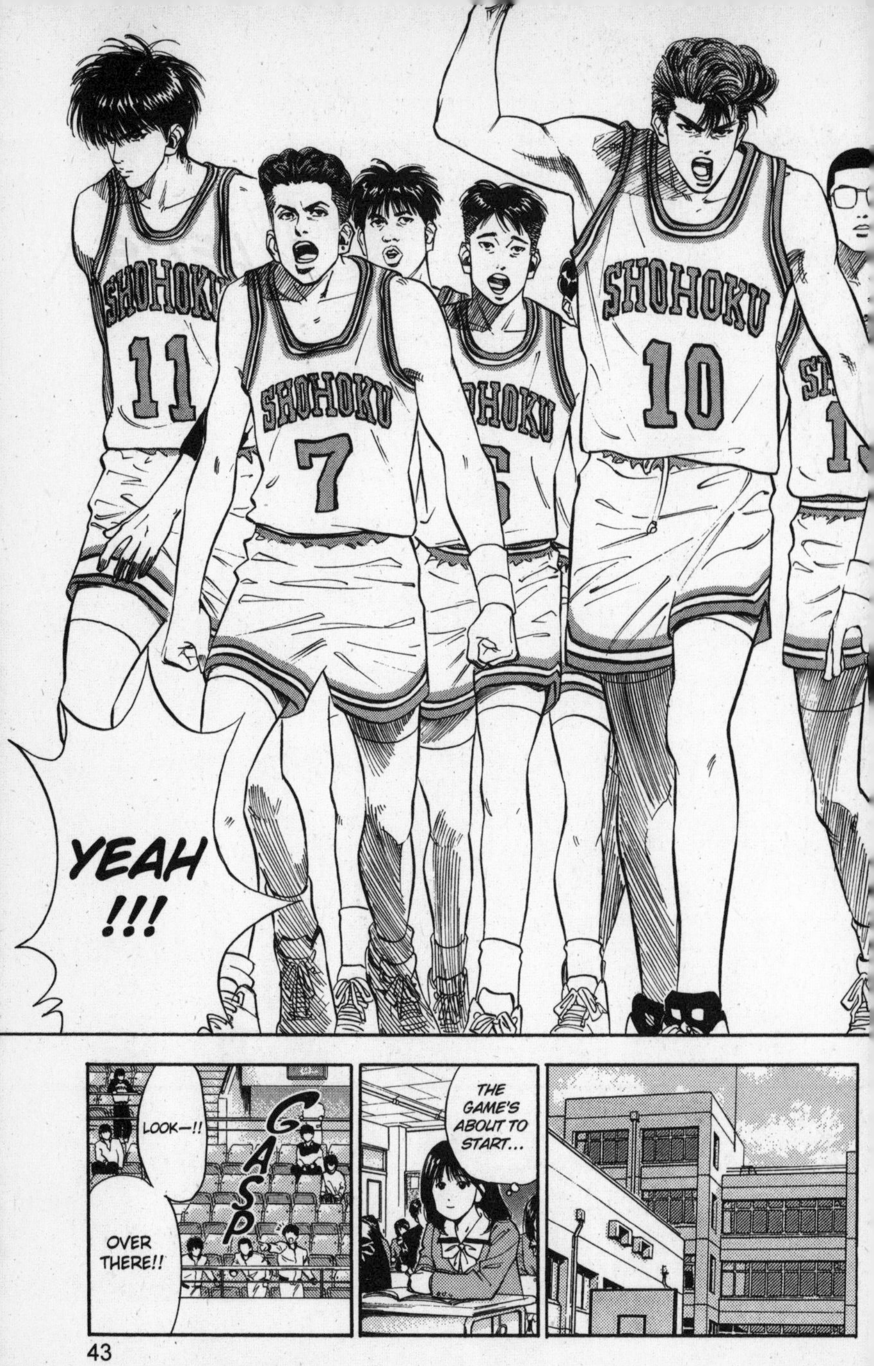

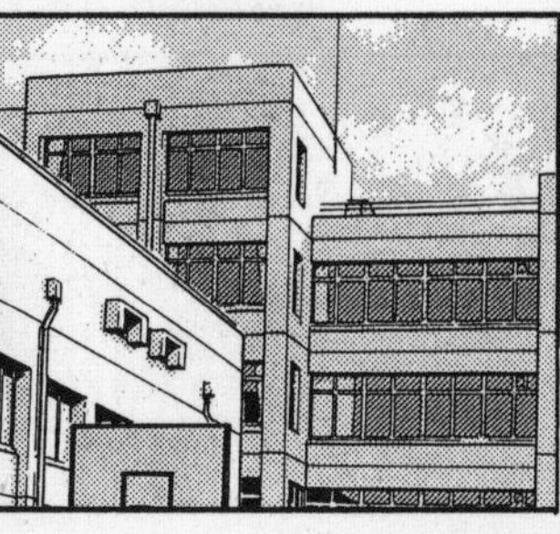

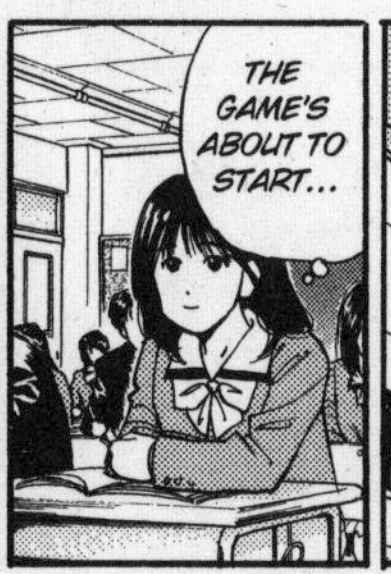
THE GAME'S ABOUT TO START...

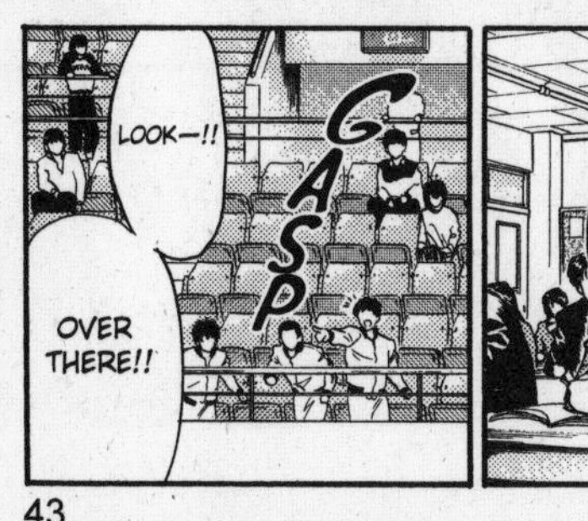
LOOK—!!
GASP
OVER THERE!!

SHUFFLE
FUSS
RYONAN!! RYONAN'S HERE!!
SHUFFLE
THEY'RE BIG!!
FUSS
FUSS
WHICH IS SENDOH?!
THAT ONE! WITH THE SPIKY HAIR!!
EEE! SENDOH!
GOTTA GET A PICTURE!
TOO BAD FOR SHOHOKU, PLAYING MIURADAI FIRST.
...
This I gotta see.
SENDOH

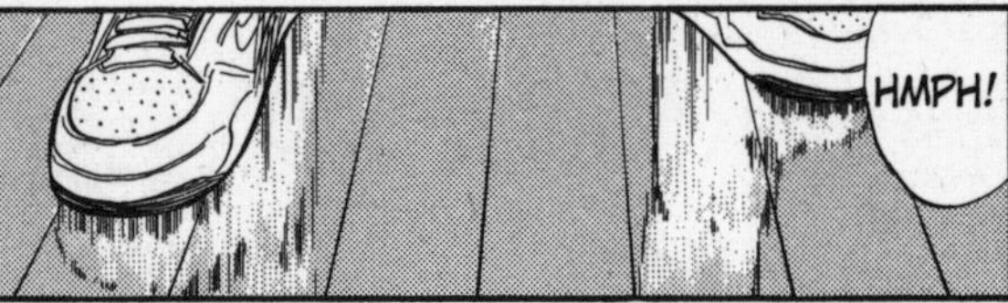

SHOHOKU'S NOTHING! JUST A STEPPING-STONE ON OUR WAY TO KAINAN.

DON

LET'S GO!!

HUH?!
GRRR
NOTHING?!
GRRRR
SLAM DUNK

#74 A TEAM OF TROUBLED TEENS

SHOHOKU VS. MIURADAI!! READY?

READY!!

Miuradai

LET'S GO!!

#74 A TEAM OF TROUBLED TEENS

YEAH!!

READ THIS WAY
THERE THEY GO!!
GAWK
CLICK CLICK CLICK CLICK CLICK
THIS IS GONNA BE GREAT!!

CHILL OUT, HIKOICHI!!
RAH
SORRY, KOSHINO!!
RAH
SHOHOKU HAS THE BALL!
RAH
WELL, DUH. AKAGI'S GOT HEIGHT ON EVERYONE BUT UOZUMI.

ALL RIGHT! LET'S DO THIS!!
PAA
PAA
LET'S GO!!

SHOHOKU'S NOT PLAYING THEIR BEST LINEUP.
RUKAWA'S ON THE BENCH ...
UOZUMI

YO, GRAMPS!
MUTTER MUTTER
YOU'RE GONNA WANT TO PUT ME IN THE GAME PRETTY SOON!
Secret weapon, yo!

...
Mm.
MM?!

HAVE YOU FORGOTTEN? YOU'RE ALL BEING PUNISHED.
HMPH!
!!

C-Coach!
!!

HEY!! GRAMPS OVER HERE IS REALLY MAD!!
BARK BARK BARK
THIS IS ALL YOUR FAULT!! DO SOME-THING!!
What did you say?!
RATTLE
GRAMPS?! SHOW SOME RESPECT!!
He's a legend!
WHAT DO YOU CARE? YOU'RE SUPPOSED TO BE ON THE BENCH, HANAMICHI!
Newbie!
HUH?! WHAT DID YOU JUST SAY TO ME?!

READ THIS WAY

FEH...
IDIOTS...
EH?!
GLARE
RUKA-WA!!

YOU THREW THE FIRST PUNCH!!
IT WAS YOU!!
BARK!
HOW DARE YOU?!
BARK!
BARK!
BARK!
I OUT-RANK YOU, DUDE. DON'T FORGET THAT!
MOVE.

HEY! SETTLE DOWN!!
We don't have time for this!

HUH?
Ayako!
The nerve of that guy...

RAH!
RAH!
RAH!
HUH?!
湘北
前半
後半
三浦台

Scoreboard: Shohoku 1st Half 2nd Half Miuradai

HU
A
HA!!
Miuradai
NICE ONE, MURASAME!!

NICE SHOT!!
MURA-SAME!!

WE'LL FINISH **THESE GUYS** OFF WITH OUR SECOND STRING.
WE NEED TO SAVE THEIR ENERGY FOR KAINAN.

I'M PULLING OUR STARTERS.
FIVE OF YOU WARM UP.

RAH
MAYBE YOU GAVE RYONAN A RUN FOR THEIR MONEY, BUT NOT US!
RAH
RAH
C'MON! WHAT'S WRONG, AKAGI?!
MIURADAI AIN'T ***SOFT*** LIKE RYONAN!!
EYES ON THE PRIZE! KAINAN'S GOING ***DOWN,*** AND WE'RE GOING TO NATIONALS!!

SNAP
SOFT LIKE RYONAN?!

AKAGI!! QUIT MESSIN' AROUND!
ROFUUUA
KICK HIS BUTT!!
SHOW 'EM HOW IT'S DONE, BOYS!
PUT RUKAWA IN!!
BOO! BOO! BOO! BOO! BOO! BOO!
YEAH! YEAH!!
RR
YOU KNOW WE'RE BETTER'N THEY ARE, AKAGI!!

YEESH...
BOO! BOO!
BOO! BOO!

THEY'RE NOT EVEN PLAYING HALF AS WELL AS THEY DID IN PRACTICE.
THEY'RE INTIMIDATED. IT'S THE FIRST BIG GAME FOR MOST OF THEM...

C'MON! FOCUS!!
WE'VE GOT THIS!

READ THIS WAY

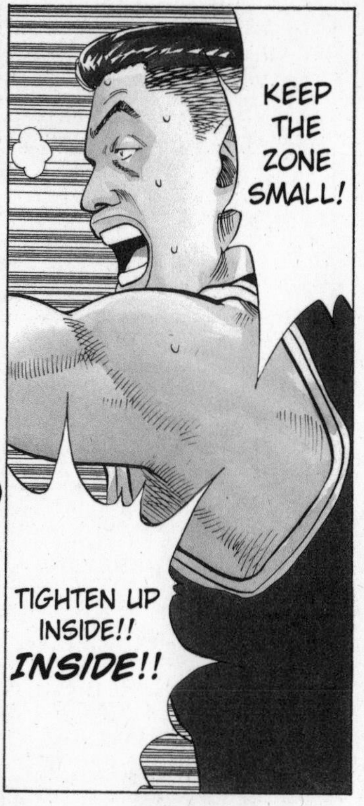

SHPP

OOF!!
HUA
SLAM
!!
FOUL!!
NUMBER 4, MIURADAI!!
FWEET

HMPH!

PFFT!
Let it go.
THAT WAS A FOUL?

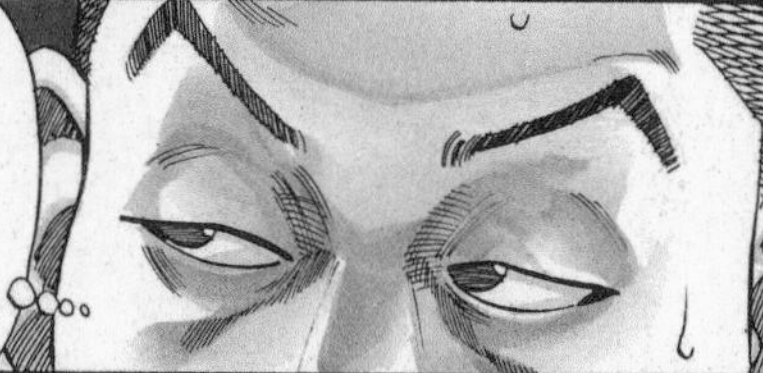
HEH. THEY'RE A ONE-MAN TEAM!

ALL WE GOTTA DO IS CONTAIN ONE GUY.

SHINK
SENDOH

GLUG GLUG
THEY COULDN'T LOSE IN THE FIRST ROUND... Could they?

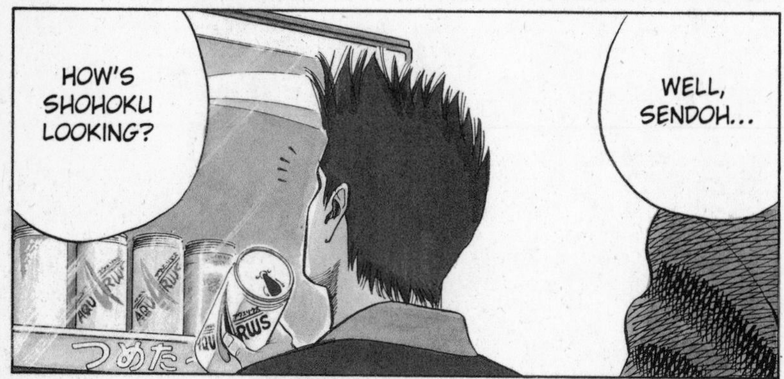
WELL, SENDOH...
HOW'S SHOHOKU LOOKING?
つめた

MAKI!!

SWISH
GOOD SHOT, AKAGI!!

RAH RAH
AKAGI'S IMPROVED HIS FREE THROWS.
MOVE!! SHUT 'EM DOWN!!
SQUEAK
SQUEAK

READ THIS WAY

'SUP, LITTLE MAN?
PAA
PAA
I'M ABOUT TO FLY RIGHT BY YOU...
!!

HEH.
SMIRK

ULP...

YES!!
SWISH
NICE SHOT !!

AW, C'MON GUYS!
FRET FRET
WHAT'RE YOU DOING?!

...

BOYS ...
HAVE YOU LEARNED YOUR LESSON?
!

NO MORE FIGHTING.
TWINKLE

COACH ...
GRAMPS?

HA HA HA! RIGHT ON, GRAMPS!!
TAP TAP TAP TAP TAP TAP
ME?! I'M A SWORN PACIFIST!
Eh?!
AH!
CUT THAT OUT !!

I WON'T FIGHT.

...I'LL TRY.

NEVER AGAIN!

RAH RAH

SHOHOKU SUBSTITUTION!!

!!

RAH RAH

DON
DON
HA HA HA!
IT'S ON NOW!!
MIGHT AS WELL GIVE UP AND SIT BACK DOWN, MIURADAI!!
DON
SHOHOKU

READ
THIS
WAY

SAKURAGI AND RUKAWA!!
RAH
OOH, MIYAGI'S BACK TOO!
HE DIDN'T PLAY LAST TIME, DID HE?
RAH
RAH

I'VE SEEN THAT GUY SOME-WHERE BEFORE ...
UOZ

WHAT NOW?
LOOK AT THESE PUNKS...
Miuradai
4
7

HMPH!
GOTTA MAKE SURE THE KIDDIES BEHAVE THEM-SELVES ...

WOW! THIS IS GONNA BE AWE-SOME!
AIDA
SHUT UP!!

SLAM DUNK

#75 WHO ARE THOSE GUYS?

HOW
ARE YOU,
SENDOH?

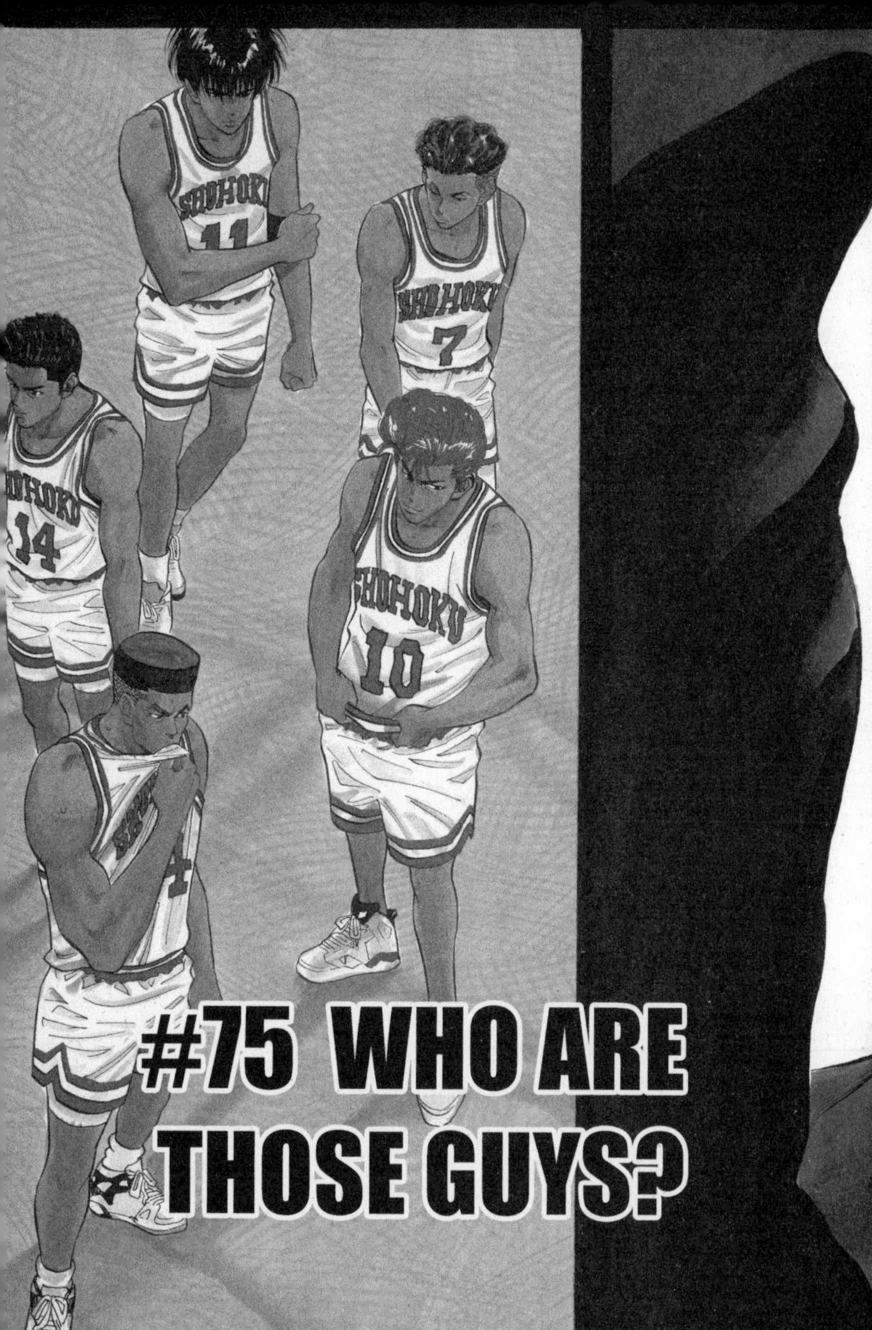
#75 WHO ARE THOSE GUYS?

I'LL TAKE NUMBER 10!!

OH YEAH?

YOU THINK *YOU* CAN GUARD *ME*?
HA...

SHOW ME WHAT YOU'VE GOT, BIG FELLA!

WHAT ?!

Grr...
WHAT?
SAKU-RAGI...
BO
!!
WHAT?!
NK
WHAT ARE YOU LOOKIN' AT? Focus!

SMIRK
DON'T LET US DOWN.

WHAT DID I DO?!

READ THIS WAY

CHECK IT OUT!!
SHOHOKU'S PLAYING FOR REAL!!

I DON'T THINK MIURADAI CAN HANDLE RUKAWA...

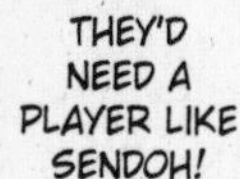
THEY'D NEED A PLAYER LIKE SENDOH!

SQUEAK
I'VE GOT NUMBER 11!!
SQUEAK
...

...
I'VE SEEN 14 BEFORE ...

I'VE GOT 14!!
SQUEAK
SQUEAK
YOU DON'T HAVE TO YELL!
Jeez!

HIKOICHI... WATCH NUMBER 7.
NUMBER 7?

HUH?!
DASH
SH
DAA
DD

READ THIS WAY
HOOGH!!
SLAM

WHOA!!

SO, WHAT'S THE STORY?

...

...

SHOHOKU'S COMING BACK.

READ THIS WAY
OOOOOO
SQUEAK
SQUEAK
SQUEAK
PAA PAAA
NUMBER 7 IS FAST !!
SO FAST!!
PAA
!!
...

YOU LITTLE TWERP !!

WAY TO GO, RYOTA !!

RYOTA!!

!!

DON'T LOOK AT ME!!
Dummy!
THRUST
I'VE GOT IT!
!!

AYAKO...♡

!!

MITSUI!!

THAT'S HISASHI MITSUI!!

SWISH

!!

YES!!
HA!

WHOA!
THEY CAUGHT UP FAST!!
RAH
RAH
RAH
WHAT HAPPENED?!

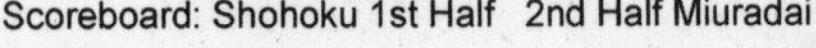
Scoreboard: Shohoku 1st Half 2nd Half Miuradai

READ THIS WAY

SHPP

THE GENIUS SAKURAGI HAS ARRIVED!!

HUH ?!
NUDGE
NUDGE

ARE YOU PUSHING ME?!
You are!
HEH HEH!

REF!
HE'S PUSHING!
Foul!
HM?

SAKURAGI!! KEEP THE BALL MOVING!!

READ THIS WAY

SQUEAK
!!

THE LOW POST IS *MINE*, I SAID!!

HUA

A DROP STEP ?!
WHEN DID HE LEARN TO DO THAT?!

YOU...

SWAT

HUH?!

READ THIS WAY

FREE THROW!!
RAH
RAH
SHOHOKU, NUMBER 10!!

EH?

Free throw?

OH NO ...
STUNNED
PLEASE TELL ME SOMEONE TAUGHT HIM HOW TO SHOOT A FREE THROW...

...
SLAM DUNK

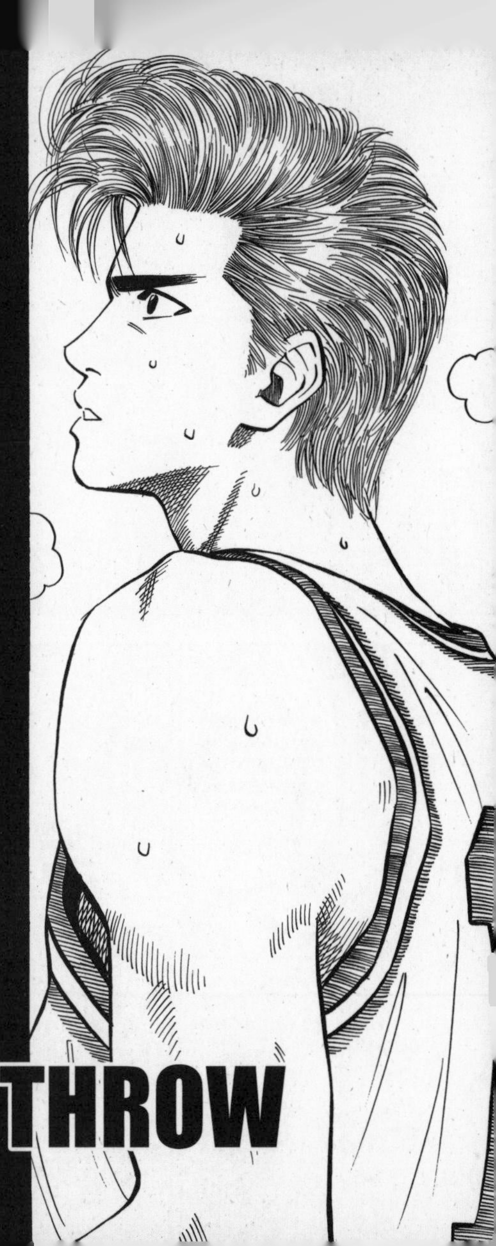

#76
FREE THROW

FREE THROW?

NUM-BER 10!

HE WON'T MAKE IT. GRAB THE REBOUND!!

WILL DO!!

!!

BONK

GRRRR

WHAT DID YOU SAY?!

STOP IT!!

LISTEN, DON'T WORRY ABOUT MAKING THE SHOT, JUST MAKE SURE YOU HIT THE RIM!!

GRAB

I'LL GRAB THE REBOUND!!

IT'S OKAY! THIS IS YOUR FIRST TIME. NO ONE EXPECTS YOU TO MAKE IT.

HM...

READ THIS WAY

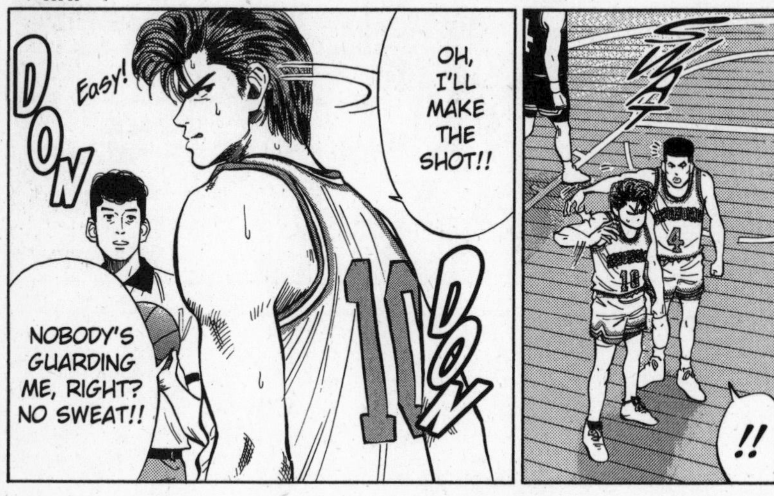
SWAT
!!
OH, I'LL MAKE THE SHOT!!
DON
Easy!
DON
NOBODY'S GUARDING ME, RIGHT? NO SWEAT!!

DON'T STEP ON THE LINE.
I KNOW!!
...Now.

TWO SHOTS!

TWO?!

ULP
...

...OOPS...
CAN'T STEP ON THE LINE.

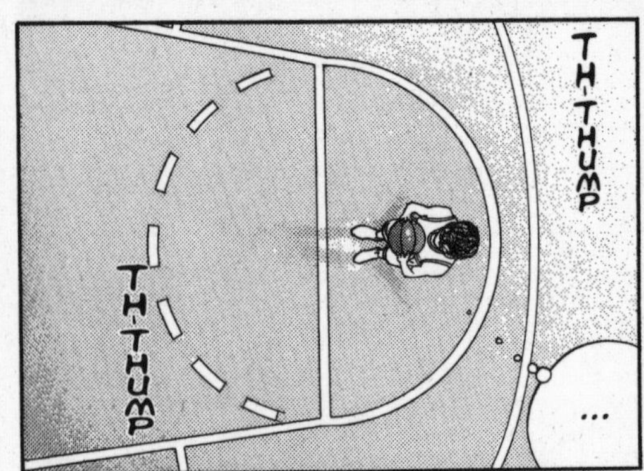
TH-THUMP
TH-THUMP
...

TH-THUMP
...
TH-THUMP

TH-THUMP
...

TH-THUMP
TH-THUMP

READ THIS WAY

THTHUMP
OH NO...
I'M NERVOUS...
Again...
THTHUMP
THTHUMP

HANAMICHI! AIM FOR THE FRONT OF THE RIM.
HUH?
!
THE FRONT OF THE RIM...
THTHUMP

NO! AIM FOR THE BACK!
KEEP YOUR EYES ON THE BACK OF THE RIM.
?!
The back?

FRONT!
BACK!
FRONT !!
BACK !!
THTHUMP
HUFF
HUFF
GRRR...
THTHUMP
THTHUMP
CHILL OUT, GENIUS!

MAKE BOTH SHOTS AND YOU *TIE THE GAME,* SAKURAGI!
IT'S ALL ON YOU!!
AIDA

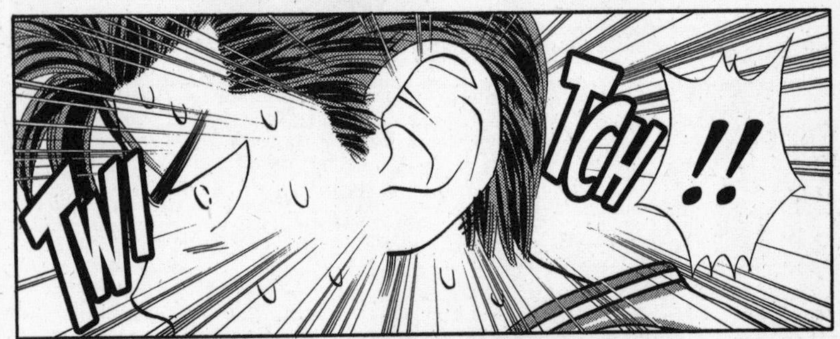
TWITCH
!!

IF I MAKE BOTH, WE'RE JUST TIED? SO IF I MISS ONE, WE'RE STILL LOSING...
TH-THUMP
TH-THUMP
CAN'T MISS!
HURRY UP AND SHOOT, DUDE.
TSK
...

READ THIS WAY

MISS MISS MISS MISS MISS MISS
MISS MISS MISS MISS
MISS MISS MISS MISS MISS MISS
MISS MISS MISS MISS MISS MISS
MISS MISS MISS MISS
MISS MISS MISS MISS
MISS MISS MISS MISS
!!

HUFF
I KNOW WHAT YOU'RE THINKING!!
Jerks!!
HUFF
MISS MISS MISS MISS MISS
HUFF

BACK!
FRONT!
HUFF
HUFF
HUFF
I HEAR YOU!!
GOT IT?
HEH HEH HEH HEH HEH HEH HEH
HUFF

HE'S GOT THIS!
NO WAY!
HEH HEH HEH!
GENIUS!
CHECK HIM OUT!
HE'S GOT THIS!
MISS!
MUTTERMUTTERMUTTERMUTTERMUT
IT'S LIKE I CAN READ THEIR MINDS!!

HWEET

FIVE-SECOND VIOLATION!!

!!

HUH?!
KOSHINO
AIDA
UEDA

RAH
CLAP
HA HA HA! SWEET!
CLAP
CLAP
CLAP
RAH
WAA
WHAT ARE YOU DOING, SAKURAGI?!
YOU GAVE THAT AWAY!!
YOU IDIOT!!
UOZUMI
RAH

(FREE THROW VIOLATION)

ONCE THE PLAYER RECEIVES THE BALL FROM THE REFEREE, HE ONLY HAS FIVE SECONDS BEFORE HE MUST SHOOT.

DR. T'S HANDY BASKETBALL TIPS

HUFF HUFF
Why is this so hard?!

I ONCE MISSED *NINE* FREE THROWS IN A ROW.

IT WAS LIKE I WAS POSSESSED.

DR. T'S BASKETBALL TALES

THIS ...
HUFF
HUFF
HUFF
HUFF
THIS IS HARDER THAN IT LOOKS!!
Idiot!

HEY, IDIOT!!
QUIT SHOWING OFF!!
BONK
AH!
!!

NO ONE HAS SHOWN YOU HOW TO SHOOT FREE THROWS YET! JUST DO WHAT I TOLD YOU.
YEAH, BUT—
ONE THING AT A TIME!!

RELAX AND SHOOT.

AIM FOR THE BACK OF THE RIM.

THE FRONT.

CLOSE YOUR EYES.

ARRGH!! BE QUIET—ALL OF YOU!!

ONE SHOT!!

SQUEAK
RUKAWA!! GET READY FOR THE REBOUND!!

SQUEAK
ON IT!
SQUEAK

OKAY...
THIS SHOULD BE EASY...
THTHUMP
THTHUMP

REBOUND!!
I-I've got it!
DING

SAKU-RAGI!! STAY LOOSE!
REBOUND!!
GET THE REBOUND!!
SQUEAK
SQUEAK
NOT A CHANCE!!

HMPH!!
OH, I AM A GENIUS IN MORE WAYS THAN ONE!
SMIRK

HUH?

WHAT THE—?!

SHU

HE HURLED IT!!

Notebook: PRIVATE

NK
HUH?!

BO

WHOA!!

!!
RUKA-
WA!!
SHOHOKU
11

!!
SLAM

READ THIS WAY

SLAP

...

PLAT

PLAT

YOU *STOLE* THAT FROM ME!!

SO?

So what?
STRUT
SLAM DUNK

#77
ROOKIE SENSATION

SCRITCH
SCRITCH

IT SHOULD BE HALF-TIME...
I WONDER WHO'S WINNING...

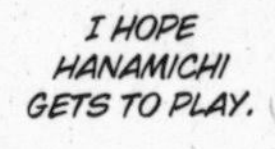
I HOPE HANAMICHI GETS TO PLAY.

...

I WONDER HOW RUKAWA IS DOING.

READ THIS WAY

IT'S THE FIRST BIG GAME FOR BOTH OF THEM.
PLAY HARD AND STAY SAFE, GUYS!

DID YOU JUST SEE THAT?!
RAH!
YOWZA!!
WHO'S NUMBER 11?!
RAH!
WHICH TEAM?
RAH!
SHOHO-KU!!
RAH!
三浦台
後半
前半
11'57
18
18

Scoreboard: Shohoku 1st Half 2nd Half Miuradai

THAT GUY'S A FIRST-YEAR!!
RAH
RAH
RAH
GRRRR
NO WAY!
THAT CAN'T BE!!
GRR
DANG IT, RUKAWA!! THAT WAS MY BALL!!
LIKE I CARE.

READ THIS WAY

WHAT THAT GUY JUST DID...
NO FIRST-YEAR DOES THAT.
UNBELIEV-ABLE...
STUNNED
MEANWHILE, SAKURAGI IS ALL OVER THE PLACE.
WHAT'S THAT GUY'S DEAL?
SAKURAGI...

HE'S ROUGH AROUND THE EDGES, BUT HIS PHYSICALITY...
IT'S BEEN A MONTH AND ALREADY HE MOVES LIKE A BALL PLAYER...
IT'S TIED UP!! LET'S GO, MURA-SAME!!
YEAH!!
FOR AN ENTIRE YEAR WE'VE DREAMED OF VENGEANCE...
OF FACING OFF AGAINST KAINAN ONCE AGAIN...
SHOHOKU WILL **NOT** DENY US THAT DREAM!!
WHOOSH

HUH ?!

OOO
WHOA! MAD HOPS!

TO
GAH!
SS
!!

!!
SH
PP
HEH

SQUEAK
YEAH !!

ALL RIGHT, LET'S GO!!

DASH DASH DASH DASH DASH DASH

FAST BREAK!!

RUKAWA IS NOT STEALING MY THUNDER THIS TIME!
TIME TO UNLEASH THE GENIUS!!
SHOHOKU
GIVE ME THE BALL!!
5

P

HUH?!

A
A

!!

GAAAAAAHH!!
SHOHOKU
11
SHOHOKU
10
SHOHOKU
7

HOHOKU
11

READ THIS WAY
TWO IN A ROW!!
HE'S EVEN BETTER THAN THEY SAID!!
T-THAT GUY...
THE ONE FROM TOMI-GAOKA JUNIOR HIGH...
IT'S KAEDE RUKAWA!!
NUM-BER 11!!

...HE'S GOOD.

WHERE WERE YOU?! YOU MISSED WHAT RUKAWA JUST DID!!
I WAS TALKING TO MAKI FROM KAINAN.
AIDA

MAKI?!
YOU TALKED TO MAKI?!

WHY DIDN'T YOU TELL ME HE WAS HERE?! I SHOULD BE WATCHING HIM!!
HE'S STILL AROUND HERE SOME-WHERE...
Ah, man!
HIKOICHI, SOME OF US ARE TRYING TO WATCH THE GAME!!

READ THIS WAY
HWEET
MIURADAI CALLS TIME OUT!!
RAH
RAH
GOOD JOB! GOOD JOB!
FWUP
WE'VE GOT THE LEAD!!
BMP BMP
GREAT PLAY, RUKAWA!!
RAH
KEEP IT UP!!
RAH
RUKAWA, EH?
HE REMINDS ME OF SENDOH LAST YEAR.
STILL...

RAH
RAH
HE'S STILL NOT QUITE THERE YET.
EXIT
RAH

READ THIS WAY

RYO!! WHY DIDN'T YOU PASS IT TO ME?!
HUH?
YOU PICKED RUKAWA OVER ME!!

LISTEN TO YOURSELF.
TRAITOR! TRAITOR! TRAITOR!

THE DEFENSE WAS ALL OVER YOU, DUMMY!
Traitor! Traitor! Traitor!
DON'T YOU SECOND-GUESS ME!!

FIGHTING AGAIN?
PLOD
NOPE!
HUG
ALL FOR ONE AND ONE FOR ALL!!

RUKAWA, YOU BIG SHOWOFF!!
I'VE HAD JUST ABOUT ENOUGH OF YOU!!

HWEET
PLAY 'EM TIGHTER!! FOUL IF YOU HAVE TO!
WE CAN'T STRUGGLE IN THE FIRST ROUND!! AM I CLEAR?!

GET RIGHT UP IN HIS *FACE*!!
MIYAMOTO!! GET YOUR BODY ON NUMBER 11!!
GOT IT!!

LET'S GO!!
YEAH!!

LISTEN UP!

WE'RE GOOD ENOUGH TO PULL THIS OFF.

KEEP FOCUSED AND WE CAN TAKE KANA-GAWA!!

THIS IS IT! TIME TO HIT 'EM WITH SOME GENIUS. I'M SICK OF BEING TOLD WHAT TO DO...
TIME TO BREAK OUT THE FORBIDDEN SLAM DUNK!!
GL
ARE

SLAM DUNK

#78 PROOF OF GENIUS

SHAA

SHAA

WORLD Coffee

SHAA
WHY DO WE HAVE TO WATCH SHOHOKU PLAY MIURADAI?
EH, JIN?
THEY'RE BOTH GOOD SCHOOLS, BUT...
I DON'T SEE EITHER AS A THREAT TO KAINAN.

READ THIS WAY

SHOHOKU'S A BIT BETTER THAN MIURADAI.
THEY'VE GOT AKAGI, MIYAGI— AND NOW RUKAWA! SHOHOKU'S WORTH WATCHING.

RUKAWA FROM TOMIGAOKA? HMPH!
THE LADIES ARE CRAZY FOR THAT KID! BAH!
BOING
FWIP
?!

KANAGAWA'S NUMBER ONE ROOKIE IS *ME*—KAINAN'S OWN NOBUNAGA KIYOTA!!
POUNCE
NOT RUKAWA!!

RAH
RAH
RAH
RAH
WONDER WHO'S AHEAD...
PFFT WHO CARES? IT'S GONNA BE A SNOOZER ANYWAY.
市体育館

H
H
YES!!

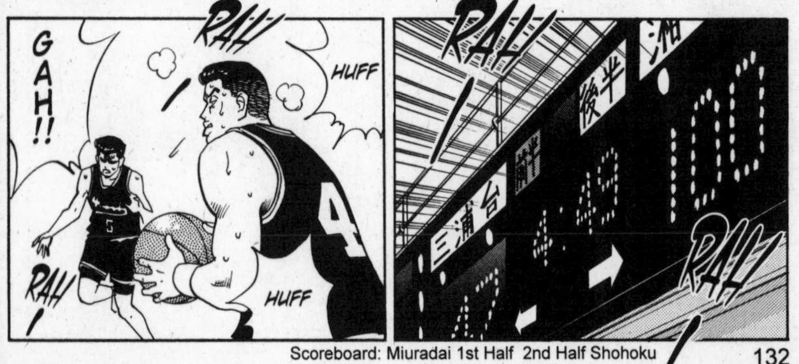

Scoreboard: Miuradai 1st Half 2nd Half Shohoku

WAH

RAH!
RAH!
...
THEY WIDENED THE GAP IN A HURRY...
AKAGI, RUKAWA AND MITSUI... THOSE THREE ARE RACKING UP THE POINTS.
AND THEY'RE STRONG ON THE BOARDS.
THEIR GUARD, MIYAGI, IS DOING HIS SHARE.
DISRUPTING THE DEFENSE AND MAKING GOOD PASSES.

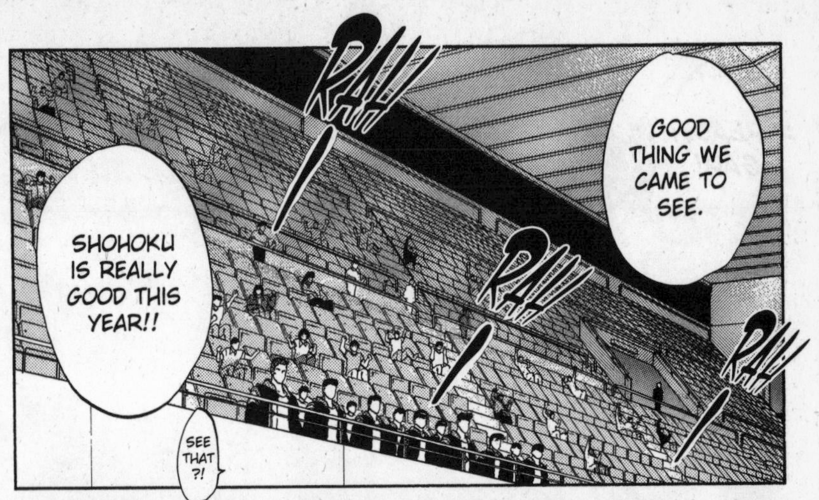
GOOD THING WE CAME TO SEE.
RAH!
SHOHOKU IS REALLY GOOD THIS YEAR!!
RAH!
RAH!
SEE THAT?!

...

PUSH
PUSH
GRR...

FUSS FUSS

I HAVEN'T SCORED A SINGLE POINT BECAUSE OF YOU!!

GET OFF OF ME ALREADY!! GAH!

FUSS FUSS

PUSH

I'M *SUPPOSED* TO GET IN YOUR WAY, YOU MORON!

FRET FRET

WILL YOU STOP TOUCHING ME?!

PUSH

THWACK

AHH!!

WRENCH

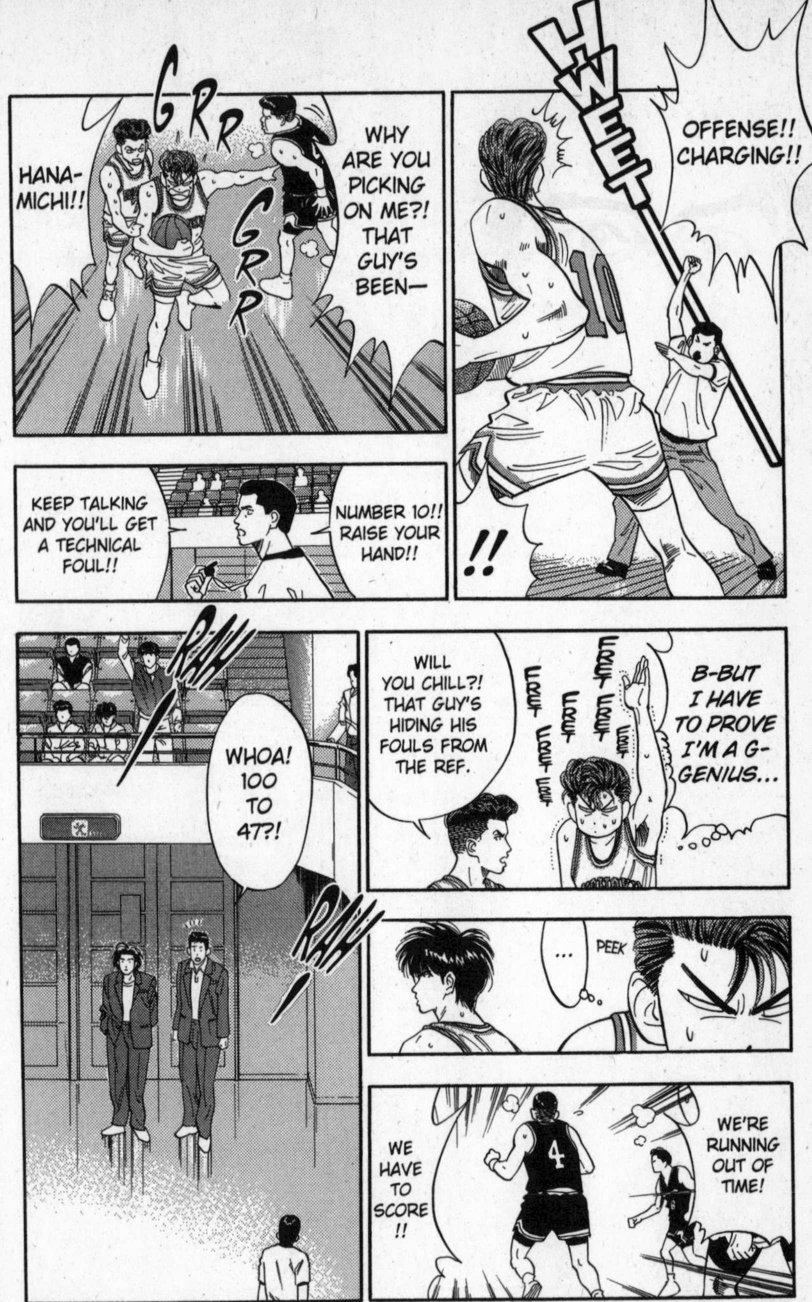
HWEET
OFFENSE!! CHARGING!!
!!
WHY ARE YOU PICKING ON ME?! THAT GUY'S BEEN—
GRR
GRR
HANA-MICHI!!
NUMBER 10!! RAISE YOUR HAND!!
KEEP TALKING AND YOU'LL GET A TECHNICAL FOUL!!
B-BUT I HAVE TO PROVE I'M A G-GENIUS...
FRET FRET FRET FRET FRET FRET FRET
WILL YOU CHILL?! THAT GUY'S HIDING HIS FOULS FROM THE REF.
RAH
WHOA! 100 TO 47?!
RAH
PEEK
...
WE'RE RUNNING OUT OF TIME!
WE HAVE TO SCORE!!

LOOK OUT, RUKAWA!!
I'M ABOUT TO PLAY THE GENIUS CARD!!

WHO'S *THAT* GUY?

SH
PP

THREE-POINTER!! GO!

HU
A

SMACK
SHOHOKU
11
!!
RUKA-
WA!!
SQUEAK
DON
DON

UUUSH
OVER HERE !!
SHFOOM
HANA-MICHI!!
SELF-PROCLAIMED BASKETBALL GENIUS HANAMICHI SAKURAGI'S OFFICIAL DEBUT!
SHPP

PAA
...WITH ONLY FOUR MINUTES REMAINING, SHOHOKU'S VICTORY WAS ALL BUT OFFICIAL.
NOT A *CHANCE*, RED!

SAKURAGI SUMMONED ALL HIS STRENGTH AND...
HUAAH

BO
!!

NK

... MISSED THE BASKET.

NOT AGAIN!!

?!

IDIOT!!

HUH!

AHHHHH
WHOA!
HWEETHWEET!
MURA-SAME!!
MURA-SAME!!

YOU DID THAT ON PUR-POSE!!
JAB JAB JAB
?!
THAT WAS ON PUR-POSE!!
WHAT?!
NO!!
I DID NOT!
MURA-SAME!!
TWITCH
TWITCH

READ THIS WAY

HUH?!
YOU! OUT!
WHAT?!
NO WAY!!

FLAGRANT FOUL※?

GAH!!
No fair!
NO, HIS FIFTH. HE FOULED OUT.

※ Requires immediate ejection.

HA HA HA HA HA!
HE'S A RIOT!!

SUPER IDIOT.

SHOHOKU HIGH SCHOOL DOMINATED MIURADAI HIGH SCHOOL WITH A SCORE OF 114 TO 51 AND ADVANCED TO THE SECOND ROUND.
WOOK
HOO
ON
O
H
RAH
RAH

I didn't do it on purpose...
Dang it...

HANAMICHI SAKURAGI'S DEBUT—ZERO POINTS SCORED, FOULED OUT WITH FOUR MINUTES TO GO. REPUTATION—FIRMLY ESTABLISHED!

FUME
SLAM DUNK

#79 MELANCHOLY GENIUS

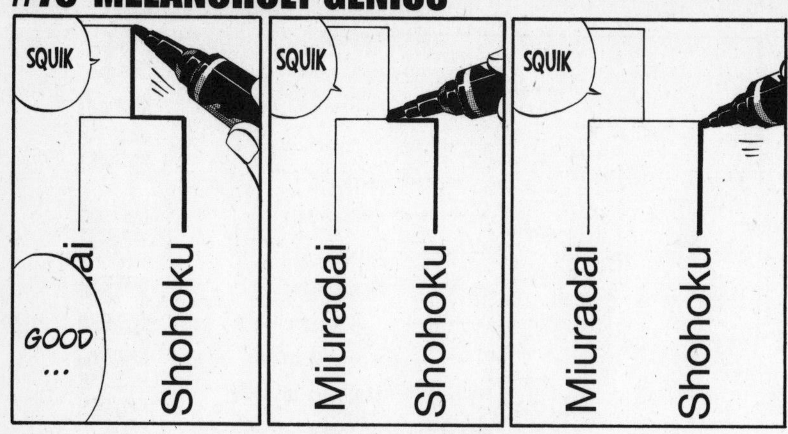

WE PASSED THE FIRST ROUND!

#79 MELANCHOLY GENIUS

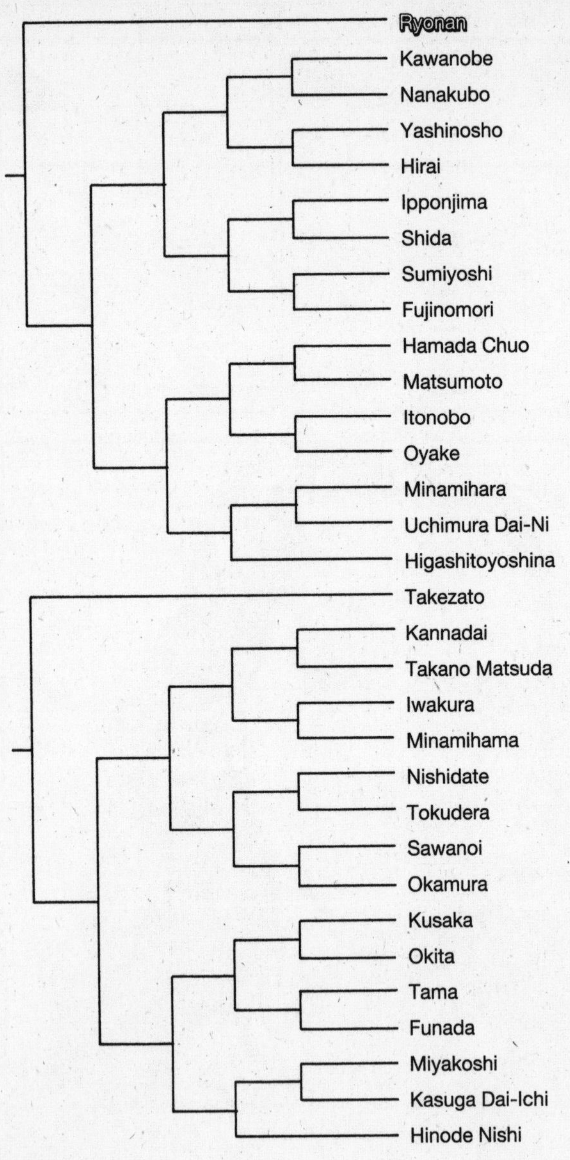
Ryonan
Kawanobe
Nanakubo
Yashinosho
Hirai
Ipponjima
Shida
Sumiyoshi
Fujinomori
Hamada Chuo
Matsumoto
Itonobo
Oyake
Minamihara
Uchimura Dai-Ni
Higashitoyoshina
Takezato
Kannadai
Takano Matsuda
Iwakura
Minamihama
Nishidate
Tokudera
Sawanoi
Okamura
Kusaka
Okita
Tama
Funada
Miyakoshi
Kasuga Dai-Ichi
Hinode Nishi

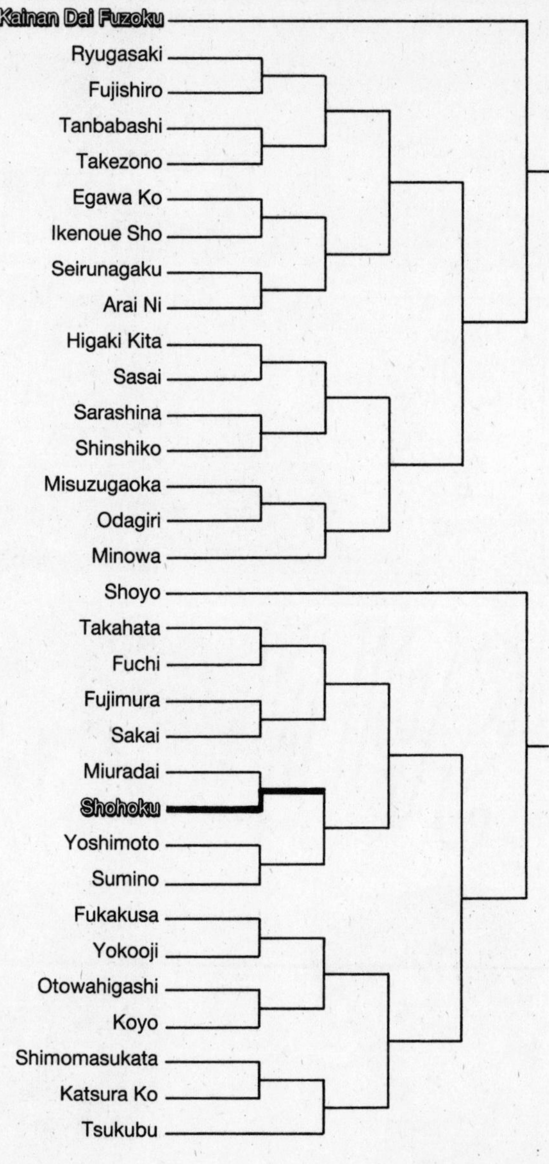
Kainan Dai Fuzoku
Ryugasaki
Fujishiro
Tanbabashi
Takezono
Egawa Ko
Ikenoue Sho
Seirunagaku
Arai Ni
Higaki Kita
Sasai
Sarashina
Shinshiko
Misuzugaoka
Odagiri
Minowa
Shoyo
Takahata
Fuchi
Fujimura
Sakai
Miuradai
Shohoku
Yoshimoto
Sumino
Fukakusa
Yokooji
Otowahigashi
Koyo
Shimomasukata
Katsura Ko
Tsukubu

SPIN !!

READ
THIS
WAY

SWOOP
URGH!!
HA!
HOP

HUH
?

THRUST
!

FLIP
...

HOP

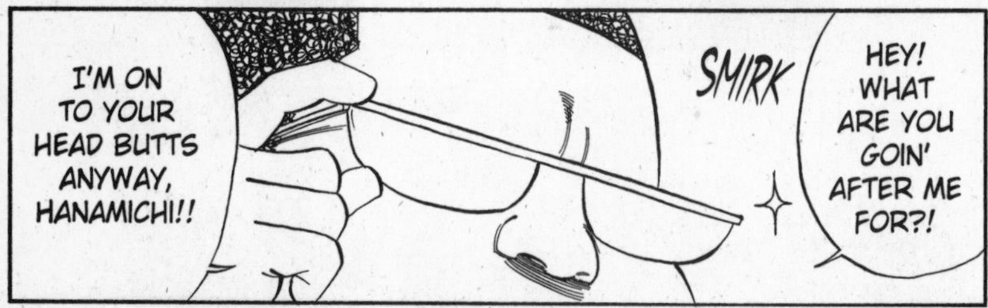
HEY! WHAT ARE YOU GOIN' AFTER ME FOR?!
SMIRK
I'M ON TO YOUR HEAD BUTTS ANYWAY, HANAMICHI!!

...

TUG
OH YEAH? ARE YOU ON TO THIS? ARE YOU?
AHH!
TUG
SMACK SMACK SMACK
Big mouth!
ARE YOU? ARE YOU ON TO THIS? ARE YOU?
YOU STILL DIDN'T SCORE A SINGLE POINT!

READ THIS WAY

Sign: Gymnasium

DON
DON
DON
WHOA!!
!!

DON
DON

BUN
BUN
BUN

...
DON
DON
DON

HE'S *HUGE*!!
WHISPER
PSS
PSS
PSS
AND *BUFF* !!

RUKAWA!
EEEE!
DON
DON
So tall...
RUKAWA-KUN!
COOL.

ULP! THEY SCARE ME.
GLARE
EEP!

AH!!

DON
DON

THAT DUDE!
FUSS
FUSS
FUSS
BIG RED THERE DUNKED ON A GUY'S HEAD!!
FUSS
FUSS
FUSS
HA HA HA!
WHAT'S WITH HIS HAIR?
HE DUNKED ON A GUY'S **HEAD!** *Insane!*
QUIVER
GAH...
QUIVER
QUIVER

LOOK ALIVE!!

LET'S TAKE IT TO 'EM!!

IT'S STARTING!!
OH? BIG RED'S NOT A STARTER?
BUZZ
WHERE'S THE HEAD DUNKER?!
BJNN
QUITE A CROWD FOR A SECOND-ROUND MATCH!
BJNN

WELL THEN...
PLOP

HEY! THOSE GUYS ARE FROM KAINAN!!
GASP
KAINAN!!

READ THIS WAY

BUZZ
KAINAN'S JIN!!
BUZZ
HE'S A SECOND-YEAR!

AND TOP-RANKED ROOKIE NOBUNAGA KIYOTA!
BUZZ

TOP-RANKED ROOKIE?
TWITCH
WHAT MAKES HIM SUCH A HOTSHOT?

...
Kiyota...

KAINAN CAME TO CHECK OUT SHOHOKU?!
FUSS
FUSS
FUSS
THEY WON'T FACE EACH OTHER UNLESS SHOHOKU MAKES IT TO THE SEMIS!!

SHOW ME WHAT YOU'VE GOT.

CHKKA
CHKKA

RUMBLE
RUMBLE
...

BIG...

...
RUMBLE
RUMBLE

I'VE PROBABLY MISSED THE FIRST HALF ALREADY...
MM?

RUMBLE
FJSS
FJSS
FJSS
!!
RUMBLE

READ THIS WAY

SHOYO
SHOYO!!

CHKKA CHKKA
CHKKA CHKKA

市体育館
Sign: Municipal Gymnasium

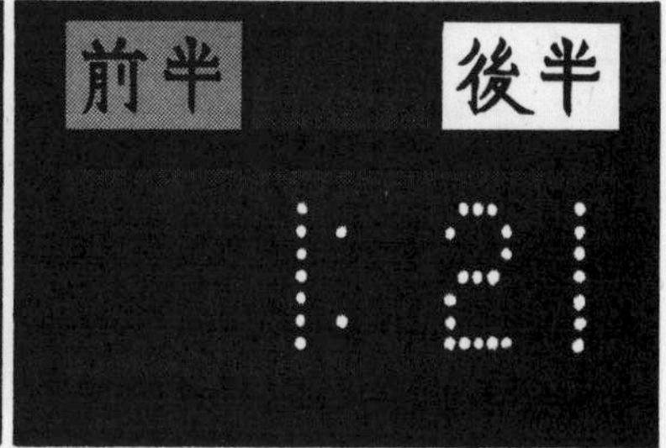
前半
後半
1:21
Scoreboard: 1st Half 2nd Half

MAN ...

Scoreboard: Sumino 1st Half 2nd Half Shohoku

READ THIS WAY

ONE MINUTE REMAINING !!
C'MON!!

ENOUGH ALREADY!!
DAA
HUFF
UHGH
HUFF
DAA
HUFF
HUFF
PLEASE LET THIS THING BE OVER WITH...

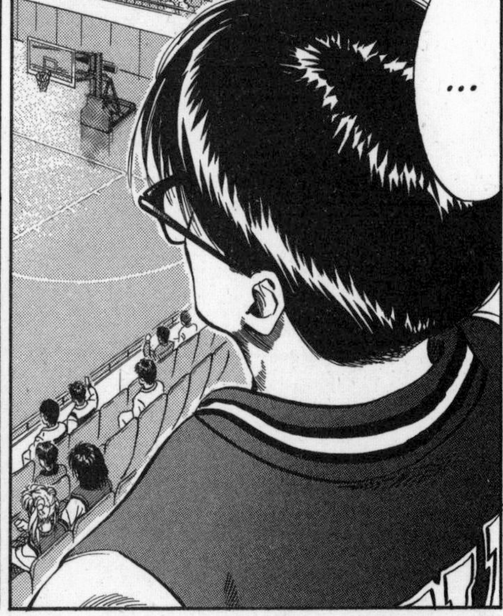
...

YOU SURE CAME A LONG WAY TO SEE THIS GAME...
!!

...
HANA-
GATA!!

READ
THIS
WAY

YES I DID, UOZUMI.
THEIR OPPONENTS ARE WEAK.

SHOYO WOULD HAVE BEEN UP BY 200 AGAINST THE SAME TEAM.

PFFT
...
MAYBE SO.
TIME'S UP!!
HOOOONK
AHHHH
YEAH! WE'RE TWO UP!

Scoreboard: Sumino 1st Half 2nd Half Shohoku

KOSHINO!
WHAT HAPPENED TO SAKURAGI? DID HE NOT PLAY?
UOZUMI!
HE DID, BUT...
HE TOOK FIVE FOULS AND GOT EJECTED...
FIGURES.

AWESOME!!
HA HA HA HA

Sign: Hard Soles Prohibited

THINK OF IT AS A LEARNING EXPERIENCE, HANAMICHI!!
THE MORE YOU EXPERIENCE, THE MORE YOU'LL LEARN!!
...
GLOOM...
SHE'S RIGHT. DON'T RUSH IT!
THAT REF WAS PICKIN' ON ME.
Unfair!
MUTTER MUTTER
THIS INDIGNITY CANNOT STAND...
SHOHOKU

READ THIS WAY

AFTER AN OVERWHELMING 160 TO 24 VICTORY IN THE SECOND ROUND, SHOHOKU WON THE THIRD ROUND CONVINCINGLY WITH A SCORE OF 103 TO 59.
THEY DREW MORE AND MORE ATTENTION WITH EACH DAY THAT PASSED.

ONCE AGAIN, (10) HANAMICHI SAKURAGI WAS EJECTED WITH FIVE FOULS.

HWEET
FOUL!
WHAT?!

I hate you...

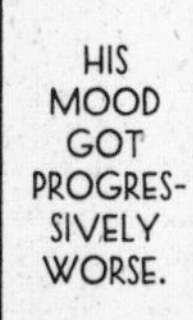
HIS MOOD GOT PROGRES-SIVELY WORSE.

IN THE FOURTH ROUND, SHOHOKU FACED THE POWERHOUSE TEAM TSUKUBU.
TSUKUBU TOOK AN EARLY LEAD, BUT...

WITH A FAST BREAK INITIATED BY A (7) MIYAGI STEAL, SHOHOKU PICKED UP THE PACE AND TSUKUBU BEGAN TO CRUMBLE.

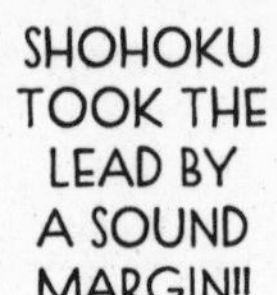
SHOHOKU TOOK THE LEAD BY A SOUND MARGIN!!

ONE ...
TWO ...
THREE ...
FOUR ...

HUH
?!

(10) SAKURAGI TOOK HIS FIFTH FOUL AND SUBSEQUENT EJECTION.

RAH
HO O N N K
RAH
RAH
YES!!

SHOHOKU ADVANCES TO THE QUARTER-FINALS WITH A SCORE OF 111 TO 79!!

READ THIS WAY

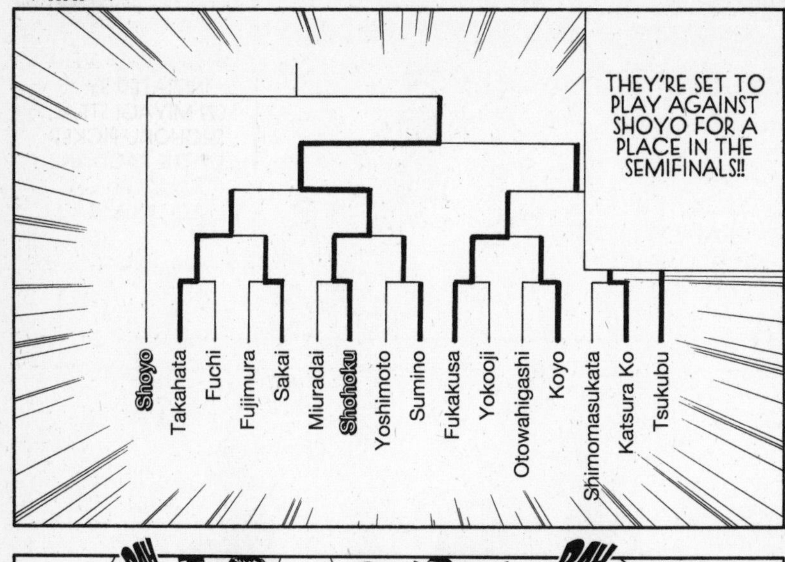
THEY'RE SET TO PLAY AGAINST SHOYO FOR A PLACE IN THE SEMIFINALS!!
Shoyo
Takahata
Fuchi
Fujimura
Sakai
Miuradai
Shohoku
Yoshimoto
Sumino
Fukakusa
Yokooji
Otowahigashi
Koyo
Shimomasukata
Katsura Ko
Tsukubu

WE'RE IN THE TOP EIGHT!!
RAH
RAH
YEP.
DAH
WOW!!

TWENTY FOULS IN FOUR GAMES... ZERO POINTS...
FOUR EJECTIONS ...

I GOT YOU TO JOIN THE TEAM...
...AND I HAVE AN EYE FOR TALENT!!
MAYBE...

GLOOM...
SORRY, HARUKO...
I'M NOT SUCH A GENIUS AFTER ALL.

GLOOM...
...
SLAM DUNK

#80
MELANCHOLY GENIUS 2

MORE.
REACH

YOU MUST BE HUNGRY. HOW MANY IS THAT?
I'M ALWAYS HUNGRY AFTER A GAME.

SO NOW YOU'RE IN THE BEST 16?
EIGHT.
CHOMP CHOMP
QUARTER-FINALS? THAT'S GREAT!

READ THIS WAY

ISN'T IT?! HONESTLY, WE CAN'T BE BEAT THIS YEAR!!
THE NEXT GAME IS SUNDAY, AND I WOULDN'T MISS IT FOR ANYTHING!

MORE!
ZOOM
Already?!
!!

DINGDONG
WHO COULD THAT BE?
PROBABLY A SALESMAN. WILL YOU GO, TAKE?
CHOMP CHOMP
JEEZ ...

HARUKO ...

DON'T BE STINGY WITH THAT RICE.

O-OKAY!!

DINGDONG
DINGDONG
I'M COMING!

CLATCH
WE'RE NOT BUYING—!
HUH? Buying what?

YOU?!
...
Sakuragi...

SWOOP
WHAT'RE YOU DOING HERE?
SHHHH!!
HARUKO MIGHT HEAR YOU!!

YOU HAVEN'T GONE HOME YET?

...

YOU'RE NOT HAVING DINNER WITH US, SO DON'T ASK!
GRR!!

I SHOULDN'T HAVE COME HERE!
THIS WAS A HUGE MISTAKE!!
?

...

CAN YOU TEACH ME HOW TO STAY IN THE GAME?

Sign: Noguchi General Hospital

SLIDE

CLEAN BILL OF HEALTH!
YOU'RE FREE TO PLAY BALL.

I'M BACK...

Sign: Noguchi General Hospital

WE PLAY SHOYO NEXT. THEY COULD HOLD THEIR OWN AGAINST KAINAN...
BUT I'M BACK, AND WE ARE *UNSTOPPABLE*!

VROOOM

SCREECH...
!!

BRM BRM
...
BRM BRM
BRM BRM
BRM BRM

READ THIS WAY

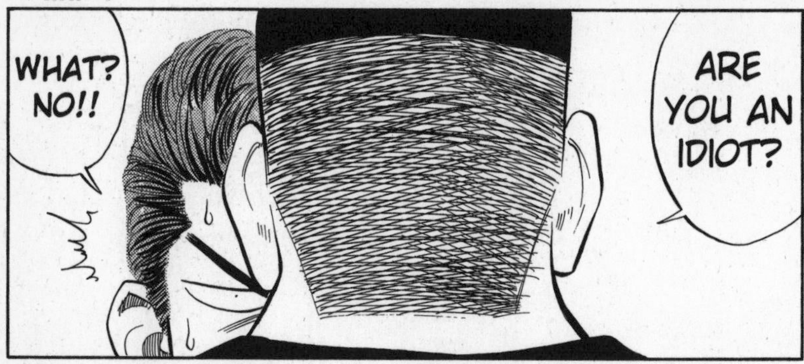
ARE YOU AN IDIOT?
WHAT? NO!!

THERE IS NO TRICK TO IT!! EVEN THE BEST PLAYERS FOUL OUT SOMETIMES.
B- BUT—!!

LISTEN, THERE'S A FINE LINE BETWEEN A FOUL AND GOOD DEFENSE.
NOTHING TAKES MORE HARD WORK THAN DEFENSE.

THAT'S WHY WE PRACTICE OUR FOOTWORK EVERY DAY.
The stuff you hate!
ER...
Footwork?

SPIN
IT'S NOT SOME SECRET I CAN JUST TELL YOU!
IT ISN'T THAT SIMPLE.

GRAB
BUT... I CAN'T GET EJECTED ANY-MORE!!
!!

...

YOU'VE TAKEN 20 FOULS ALREADY. WHAT HAVE YOU LEARNED?
HOW FAR COULD YOU GO WITHOUT HEARING THE WHISTLE? WHEN WAS IT A FOUL? THINK ABOUT THAT.

THEN DON'T GET BEATEN BY YOUR MAN.
YOU CAN'T ALWAYS GO FOR THE FLASHY MOVES!
OOF...

STUPID GORI... THINKS HE'S SO GREAT!
MUTTER
MUTTER
ALWAYS TALKIN' DOWN TO ME...

...

I'M A GENIUS!
A BONA FIDE BASKETBALL GENIUS!
I just know it!

PAAA
PAAA
PAAA
HUH?

?
PAAA
PAAA

WOULDN'T GIVE UP EASY, HUH? THEY DON'T USUALLY LAST THAT LONG.
You scare them!
CHOMP
CHOMP

YEAH ...
THIS ONE WAS BRAVER THAN MOST.

THAT'S WHAT MAKES HIM WORTH THE TROUBLE.
?

HE MIGHT JUST HOLD THE KEY TO VICTORY AGAINST SHOYO.

野口総合病院
HIM AND ONE OTHER...

?
REALLY ?
?
?

Sign: Noguchi General Hospital

TETSUO!!

...

I HAD A CHECKUP FOR MY KNEE.
WHAT'S WITH THE HAIR?

YOU LOOK LIKE A JOCK.
FLICK

...
I KID ...
IT LOOKS GOOD.
GRIN
TETSUO ...
EEE OOO
UH OH. HERE THEY COME...
I THOUGHT I LOST THEM.
OOOO EEEEEEE OOOOO
I HATE WEARIN' A HELMET.
V-V ROOM

BRM
LATER...
BRM
...SPORT.
BRM
VROOOOOOM
OOOO
EEEE
EEEE
OOO
EEE
YOU ON THE BIKE!! PULL OVER!!
EEEE
PULL OVER RIGHT NOW!
OOOOOOO
...
EEEE
EEE
PULL OVER!!
HEY!!
LATER...
TETSUO.
MY HEAD DOES GET COLD AT NIGHT...
PAT
PAT

PAA
CREAK
WHO IS THAT?
PAA
PAA
PAA
PAA
!!
SHOHOKU
11

RUKAWAWA!!
PAA PAA
PAA PAA
HUAH
PAAAA

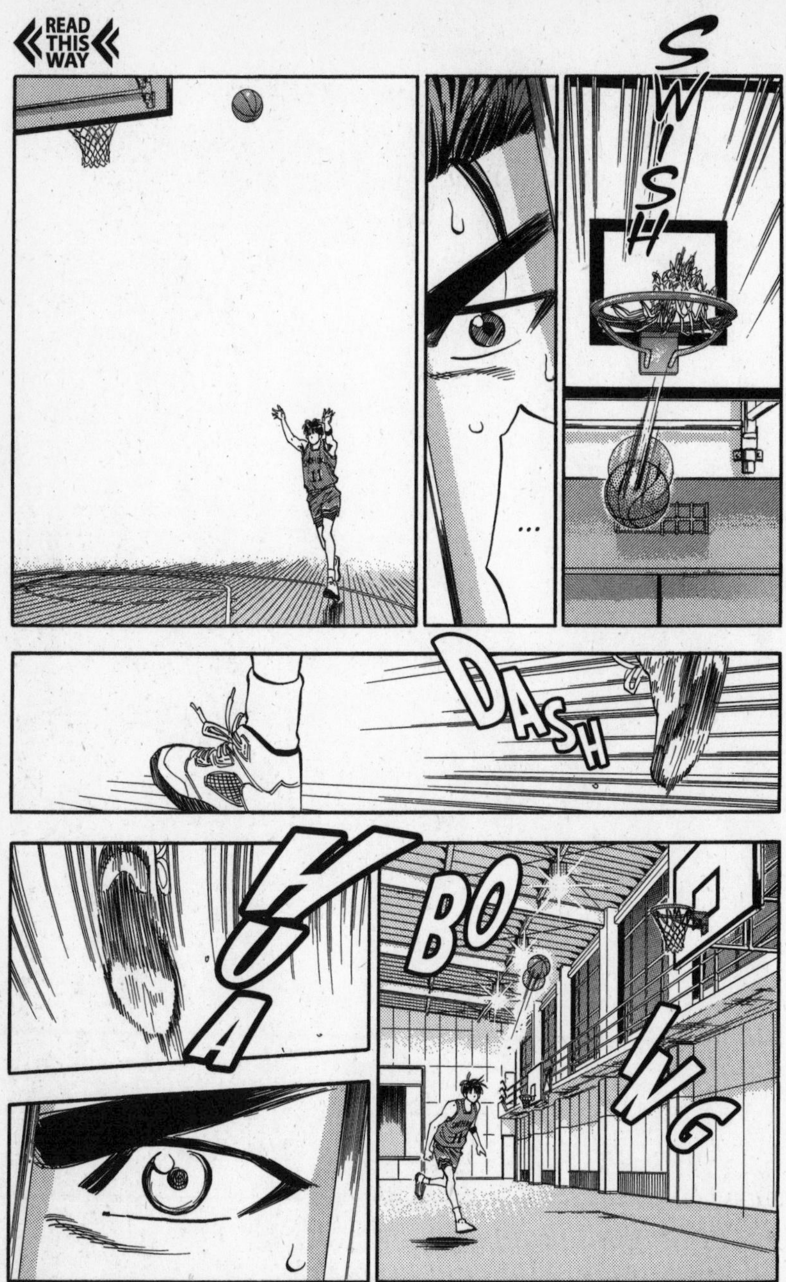
READ THIS WAY
SWISH
...
DASH
HUOA
BOING

SLAM

READ THIS WAY

PHEW...

HEY!!

TO BE CONTINUED!

Coming Next Volume

Sakuragi and his teammates appear to be building momentum as they advance into the Final Four, but their next opponent, the squad from Shoyo, is one of the tallest teams in the tournament. And while Shoyo's considerable height advantage throws a bit of a scare into the boys from Shohoku, their resolve stands firm. And what's this? Sakuragi's placed in the starting five! Has Coach Anzai lost his jolly mind?!

SLAM DUNK

Kevin Garnett

Hey basketball fans! Welcome to the Slam Dunk Omake-Dome, where basketball neophytes and street gamers alike learn how to ball like the pros. Today we welcome one of the fiercest competitors in the game, Kevin Garnett, into the fray, and learn a thing or two about putting together impregnable team defense. Caution, sweat and hard work required!*

Blood, Sweat and Tears

"Anything is possible!" Hanamichi might come up with a phrase like that, but for someone who actually talks the talk and walks the walk, look no further than Boston Celtics forward Kevin Garnett, who uttered those words after he led his team to a stirring NBA Finals victory over the Los Angeles Lakers in 2008. Kind of ironic, considering his favorite team as a kid was the Lakers!

"Anything is possible" are the words the man known as "KG" lives by—growing up in a poor family in South Carolina, his rise to stardom is the result of sheer drive and determination. As a young high schooler he often found himself playing against older and bigger kids, and the tough training served him well when he transferred to Farragut High School in Chicago, where his hoops career took off. At the McDonald's All-American game, which pits the best high school ballers in the country against each other, he walked off with the John Wooden Award as the game's outstanding player and gained the notice of the Minnesota Timberwolves, where he spent the first 12 seasons of his career.

Garnett was a human highlight reel during his Minnesota career, playing with the gold medal-winning U.S. Olympic basketball team in 2000 and earning NBA Most Valuable Player honors in 2003, but the one goal he coveted most—a championship trophy—didn't come along until the 2007–8 season, when he was traded to the Celtics and was the catalyst that fueled the team's run to the title. He wears a tattoo with the words "blood, sweat and tears," and no other three words can better describe his approach to the game. At least now he can say that the "tears" were the tears of joy he cried when he won the championship!

Team Player

If you have to describe KG in one word, it would be "intensity." A seven-footer with outstanding quickness and a giant wingspan, he goes full tilt every minute of every game, and has the ability to both mix it up down low with the big bodies and take it outside for a sweet jump shot.

KG's calling card is his vocal leadership and selfless play. Here's a player who takes just as much pleasure from helping a teammate out on defense—or getting a timely rebound or blocked shot—as he does from anything he does on offense. As the man himself says, "I have never been a personal stat guy… I overlook all those things and focus on team accomplishments." His ability to rally his teammates and lead by example has transformed the Celtics into one of the NBA's elite teams, not to mention one of the best defensive squads around. Speaking of which…

CAREER SEASON AVERAGES

Year	Team	G	GS	MPG	FG%	3P%	FT%	OFF	DEF	RPG	APG	SPG	BPG	TO	PF	PPG
95-96	MIN	80	43	28.7	0.491	0.286	0.705	2.2	4.1	6.3	1.8	1.1	1.6	1.38	2.36	10.4
96-97	MIN	77	77	38.9	0.499	0.286	0.754	2.5	5.6	8.0	3.1	1.4	2.1	2.27	2.58	17.0
97-98	MIN	82	82	39.3	0.491	0.188	0.738	2.7	6.9	9.6	4.2	1.7	1.8	2.34	2.73	18.5
98-99	MIN	47	47	37.9	0.460	0.286	0.704	3.5	6.9	10.4	4.3	1.7	1.8	2.87	3.23	20.8
99-00	MIN	81	81	40.0	0.497	0.370	0.765	2.8	9.0	11.8	5.0	1.5	1.6	3.31	2.53	22.9
00-01	MIN	81	81	39.5	0.477	0.288	0.764	2.7	8.7	11.4	5.0	1.4	1.8	2.84	2.52	22.0
01-02	MIN	81	81	39.2	0.470	0.319	0.801	3.0	9.1	12.1	5.2	1.2	1.6	2.83	2.27	21.2
02-03	MIN	82	82	40.5	0.502	0.282	0.751	3.0	10.5	13.4	6.0	1.4	1.6	2.79	2.43	23.0
03-04	MIN	82	82	39.4	0.499	0.256	0.791	3.0	10.9	13.9	5.0	1.5	2.2	2.59	2.46	24.2
04-05	MIN	82	82	38.1	0.502	0.240	0.811	3.0	10.5	13.5	5.7	1.5	1.4	2.71	2.52	22.2
05-06	MIN	76	76	38.9	0.526	0.267	0.810	2.8	9.9	12.7	4.1	1.4	1.4	2.37	2.71	21.8
06-07	MIN	76	76	39.4	0.476	0.214	0.835	2.4	10.4	12.8	4.1	1.2	1.7	2.70	2.42	22.4
07-08	BOS	71	71	32.8	0.539	0.000	0.801	1.9	7.3	9.2	3.4	1.4	1.2	1.94	2.30	18.8
08-09	BOS	57	57	31.1	0.531	0.250	0.841	1.4	7.1	8.5	2.5	1.1	1.2	1.58	2.25	15.8
09-10	BOS	12	12	30.3	0.510	0.000	0.727	1.5	5.8	7.3	2.5	1.2	0.9	1.42	2.17	13.5
Career	--	1,067	1,030	37.5	0.496	0.283	0.782	2.6	8.4	11.0	4.3	1.4	1.6	2.47	2.50	20.1
All-Star	--	11	9	22.2	0.515	0.000	0.875	2.2	4.8	7.0	3.2	1.4	0.8	1.55	0,91	13.6

D-fense! D-fense!

The backbone of any winning team is good defense. What's the definition of good defense? It's all the stuff we've talked about in previous volumes of *Slam Dunk*—the rebound, the blocked shot, the steal—applied throughout the entire team.

There are different ways out there to play team defense—you may go man-to-man (one player covering one opposing player), you may go zone (where you guard a certain area, or zone, of the court), or you may have a combo of both. But the keys below are the same no matter whom you're guarding or what defense you're playing. Take them to heart and soon you and the rest of your team will be shutting down your opponents!

Keys for Team Defense

1. "E" for Effort
Defense is more than a skill—it's an attitude. Commit yourself to playing good D every second. No matter where you are on the court, even if it looks like you're out of the play, keep hustling. It can mean the difference between a good and great defensive performance.

2. "C" for Communication
This is where the "team" in "team defense" comes in. You're not alone out there—you have teammates to back you up (and vice versa). The best defensive teams always communicate and coordinate with each other during play on the court, so keep the chatter up! A quick shout to a teammate can lead to a great defensive stop.

3. "T" for Transition
Transition defense happens when the other team is hustling the ball down the court on offense. If they beat you to the other end it leads to a quick dunk or basket, so keep between other players and the basket as much as you can. (This also ties into "E" for Effort.)

4. "J" for Jump to the Ball
We don't mean jumping like jumping straight up—many times you'll have to maneuver past other players when the ball is passed around. The quickest, easiest way to do it is to "jump" to where the ball is headed. This puts pressure on the ball handler and keeps you in good position to make a play. Practice getting your timing and range down on your "jumps."

5. "Q" for Quick Hands and Feet
Defense is all about anticipation and reaction—if you can anticipate the play your opponent is about to make and can react in time, chances are you'll make a big play. Practice swatting at the ball (without fouling the other player, of course), moving quickly, and closing in on your opponent and the ball. Swarming, persistent D will fluster your opponents and lead to turnovers!

Bonus "Tip": "H" for Help Defense

Sometimes one of your teammates might be guarding an opposing player and the opposing player shakes free. The only thing standing between him and an easy basket is "help" defense, where another teammate steps in to defend. When guarding your man, keep one foot in the lane and one foot outside the lane facing the player you're defending, and keep an eye on the ball. This is prime position to help defend against other players when necessary. Quick-reaction help defense catapulted the Celtics to an NBA championship in 2008, when they held the Lakers to play-off lows in rebounding and field goal percentage!

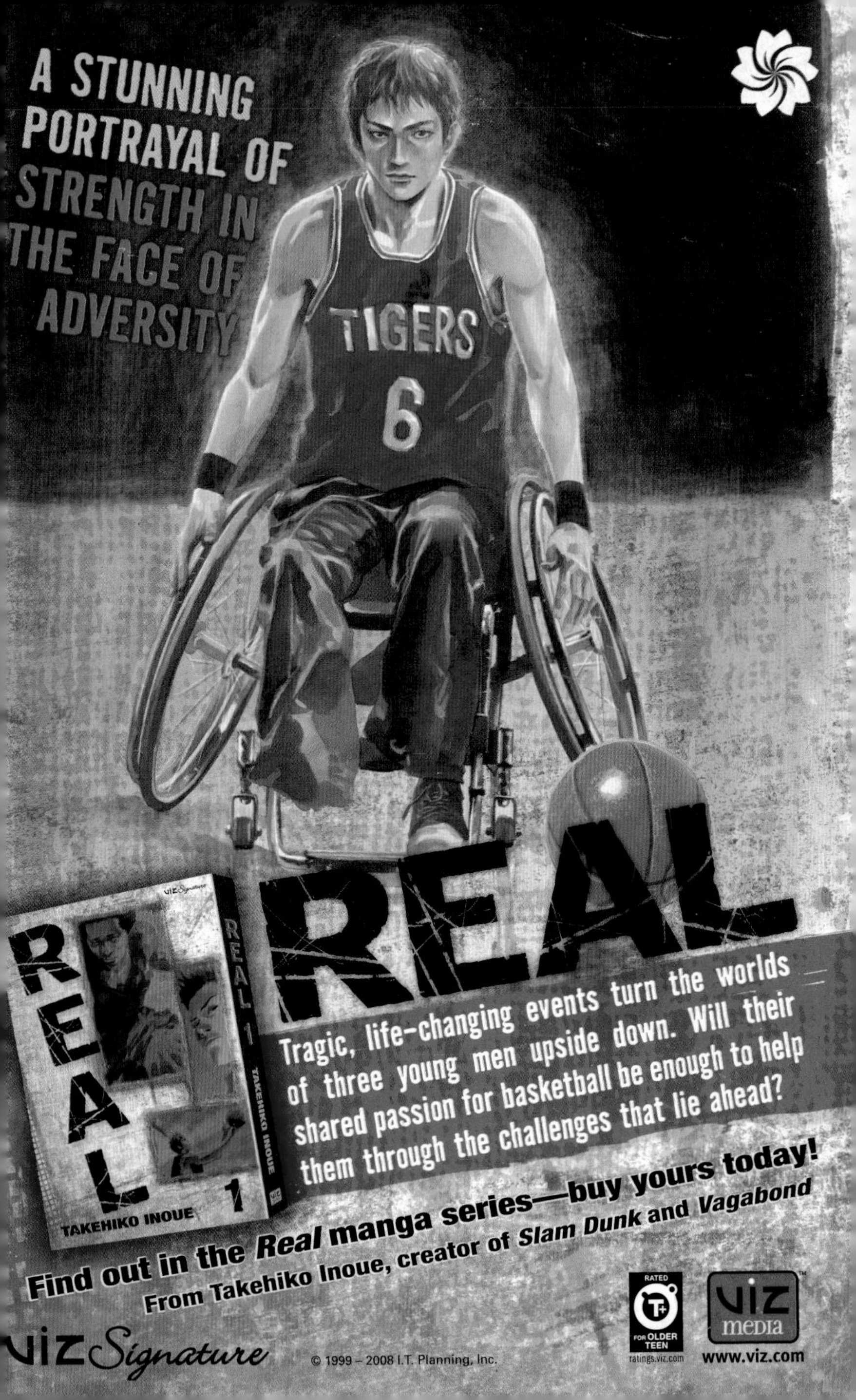